I am a 27 year old Primary Teacher from Ireland. I graduated from St Patrick's College Drumcondra with a Bachelor of Arts in Music and English and continued to complete a Postgraduate Diploma in Primary Education at the University of Glasgow. I have spent my life teaching children of all ages in countries across Europe, Asia and South America.

I myself have suffered from Depression and Anxiety at different points of my life and I want to use my experience to educate the future generation about positive mental health. Through my different roles in teaching, leadership and management, part of the Special Educational Needs Department and as a Child Protection and Safeguarding Officer, I have observed first hand the challenges that our children are facing and how poorly they are equipped to deal with them. I am a firm believer in the importance of children developing resilience and that the first step to getting there is by helping them recognise, understand and appropriately deal with their emotions.

I really hope that this book can help children to feel confident in expressing their emotions and develop a strong sense of positive mental health.

Is fearr an tsláinte ná na táinte.

Emma Cahill

Text © 2019 by Emma Cahill
Illustrations © 2019 by Paul Nugent
All rights reserved, Including the right of
reproduction in whole or in part in any form.

First edition 2019
ISBN:9781691280629

UNDER THE MASK

Dedicated to my fantastic niblings
Eva, Faye, Léa and Aaron - My real life Superheroes!

From day one, my mantra has been 'If this book helps even just one child, it will have been worth the time and effort.' Anyone who has helped support this book in any way is also responsible for helping that child. So, a big thank you to my troop of proofreaders for giving me the courage to speak up and keep going. It has been heartwarming to see how many people are willing to support Mental Health Awareness. Ireland may be a small country but we are fierce and determined. Let's end the stigma and start teaching our smallest members that it's OK not to be OK!

WRITTEN BY
EMMA CAHILL

ILLUSTRATED BY
PAUL NUGENT

www.emmacahill.ie

www.paulnugentillustration.com

Olly is tall, and thin with rosy cheeks.

He's nine, turning ten in a couple of weeks.

He loves water fights with the garden hose,

And laughing until milk comes out of his nose!

You can see his tonsils when he starts to giggle,

And his toothy smile is a big red squiggle.

But lately, Olly's not such a happy guy.

He feels different and heavier, but doesn't know why.

He wants to *feel* strong again, to bring his happiness back.

So he visits the Superheroes, who live down the track.

'I need your help, I need advice, everything feels all wrong.

I want to *feel* like me again. Please help me to be strong!

I have these funny feelings that keep rising in my chest.

I'm keeping them a secret. What do you suggest?'

Being strong does not mean
hiding how you feel,
It's dealing with your feelings
and accepting that they're real.
Everyone feels anger
and everyone feels sad,
Everyone feels worried,
it's normal, it's not bad.
It's important that we talk about it
and learn some ways to deal,
And remember:

'IT'S OK
TO FEEL
EXACTLY
HOW YOU
FEEL!'

But you are rugged heroes,

You don't ever suffer.

Am I the only one who struggles?

You three seem so much tougher.

Oh dear Olly, how wrong you are!

Everyone struggles at times.

Life is not an easy road;

it's filled with dips and climbs.

Even the strongest athletes tumble.

Even the sturdiest materials break,

Even the toughest cookies crumble.

But it's all for learning's sake.

We're superheroes, who wear no masks
We do not need to hide,
The weather that's within us,
The battles from inside.
We're superheroes, who wear no masks
To hide or to conceal
The foggy world of feelings
The heaviness we feel.

If we're feeling like a cup, that has been overfilled.
We activate our superpowers, and let ourselves be spilled.
We do it in a safe way, that doesn't hurt our heart.
You have these powers too, let us show you how to start!

Blaze

I'm a pretty strong girl -
I've got my Superhero suit.
I want to seem grown up and tough,
like Grandad's leather boot.

But I often feel quite angry, like a balloon about to pop.
I feel my blood makes bubbles and they rise up to the top.
My muscles feel much stronger and my hands curl up so tight.
I need to shout and get it out, I'm ready for a fight!
I slam the doors, I clench my fists.
My face feels hot like fire,
When people tell me to 'CALM DOWN',
The bubbles just rise higher.

It's then that I remember, I'm the one who holds the key

To unlock my ability for ME to control me.

Tricks that I've learned and tools to help succeed

Superpowers to activate, anytime I need.

When I feel like a volcano and I think I might explode

I activate the Bs to take a calmer road.

I pay attention to my **BREATHING**,
breathe in and out for five.

I **BOUNCE** or jump or dance,
or shake and move and jive.

When I'm feeling calmer, I **BRAINSTORM** how I feel,
I search for words to express myself and find safer ways to deal.

Anger can be important too, it helps us stay headstrong.
It helps us see unfairness or help us right what's wrong.

Rustle

I'm a pretty confident guy -

I've got my Superhero gear.

I want to seem so brave and fierce

whenever I sense fear.

But I often feel worried, like there's butterflies in my chest.
It makes me feel quite queasy and I cannot do my best.
My tummy starts to flutter, my throat feels blocked by worry.
Everything seems much harder and my breathing seems to hurry.
I feel myself start trembling and then I start to shake
It's like I'm in a nightmare but yet I cannot wake.
It's like a drum that's beating, fast between my bones.
It's all that I can think about, so many big unknowns.

It's then that I remember, I'm the one who holds the key

To unlock my ability for ME to control me.

Tricks that I've learned and tools to help succeed

Superpowers to activate, anytime I need.

When I feel like a hurricane, That's shaking and rumbling,

I activate the R's to halt it all from tumbling.

I **RETHINK** why I'm worried -
is there really lots to fear?

I **REPLY**, I say "No, that's not true!",
that's what worry needs to hear.

I **RELAX** by breathing deeply
and using music, art and sport. And
I talk to someone close to me, for
comfort and support.

Worry can be important too,
it can keep us out of harm.
It can warn us about danger,
like a siren or alarm.

Crash

I'm a pretty happy guy -

I've got my Superhero grin.

I almost seem as happy

as when Santa Claus drops in.

My head becomes all fuzzy
and my lip begins to quiver.
It's difficult to speak
and my tears flow like a river.

I've forgotten how to smile,
all I can do is weep.
My energy is gone
and I want to go to sleep.
Nothing makes me happy now,
I'm never bright or cheery.
I've stopped playing with friends,
I'm just quiet, tired and teary.

It's then that I remember, I'm the one who holds the key

To unlock my ability for ME to control me.

Tricks that I've learned and tools to help succeed

Superpowers to activate, anytime I need.

When I feel like a flood and a sea of tears comes rushing

I activate the C's to ease the sadness gushing.

I **CHAT** with someone close to me and share what's going on

I **CREATE** something new for me like a painting, dance or song.

This will **PASS**

I **CHANGE** what's in my control and wave goodbye to the past. Keep saying 'This will pass' and remember sadness doesn't last.'

Sadness can be important too, as it tells us we're in pain. It tells us to change something so that it doesn't happen again.

So just like fire, water and air, my emotions have such power.

It's how I choose to deal with them that makes them sweet or sour.

But what happens if these feelings last more than a day?

If the worry never stops or the tears won't go away?

If it's difficult to smile and you always feel alone,
Or if you feel like you are carrying all your problems on your own.
Just know that you are NEVER in this world without a friend,
There's always someone to help bring your sadness to an end.
Talk to an adult, that you trust and do not fear.
Be honest about what's going on and let them lend an ear.
Together, you can find a way to bring the sun back out,
To help you see the light and let them hear you shout!
You'll feel like you again, you know, feelings do not last.
You just need to have some patience, as this may not happen fast.
It might take time to gain control, until the feeling clears.
But you have strength to overcome your sadness and your fears.
Your future holds new friends, delicious cakes and super games.
You'll light this world up and shine so bright, it might go up in flames!

Thank you Superheroes, for giving me the key.

To unlock my ability for ME to control ME.

I have powers within me, to soothe and to heal,

And I know that it's Ok to feel exactly how I feel.

I have dreams to follow and I have goals to score,

I have battles I will win, and I'll enjoy much more.

So let's be kind to our minds, and be our OWN best friend,

This is only the beginning, this is **NOT** the end!

ENDORSEMENTS

'I cannot recommend this book highly enough! Gorgeous, subtle way of teaching children valuable coping mechanisms for everyday life. Emma highlights the importance of talking about your emotions and reminds children that everybody has emotions, it's about learning healthy ways to deal with them. It's beyond beautiful to see these wonderful messages being passed to our younger generation.'
- Keith Duffy, Singer-Songwriter

'Emma is highly experienced and an incredibly talented writer. She tackles the most important and relevant topic of mental health and emotional wellbeing in a fun, accessible and creative way. Her book "Under the Mask" is a much needed addition to children's literature and will be a great support for helping children to develop their awareness of, and manage, a range of emotions. I can't wait to use it in my assessment and therapy work with children.'
- Deirdre Hogan, Music Therapist (Early years Intervention)

'A wonderfully accessible resource that normalises emotions in a fun and engaging way. Olly and the superheroes will help children manage their feelings by teaching practical skills that can be used in everyday life.'
- Dr Clodagh Feehan, Child Clinical Psychologist

'This book is a Mental Health Masterpiece! All children need to have this in their collection. Relatable Superheroes teaching kids simple steps to build their resilience while teaching valuable lessons about their Mental Health is heartwarming and essential for the world we live in.'
- Marty Guilfoyle, Broadcaster and DJ

'Emma has tapped into the interest of a lot of children by developing her superhero characters. Using these beautifully created characters to explore the themes of emotional well-being and feelings is a brilliant way of engaging her young audience. As a teacher and Art Therapist, books like this are vitally important to engaging and supporting the children I work with. This book is ideal! These colourful and fun superhero characters will no doubt, support lots of young boys and girls. Thank you for creating such a valuable resource, Emma!'
- Helena Mullooly, Primary School Teacher, Art Therapist & Children's Mindfulness Practitioner

'Unfortunately, there is a significant lack of resources to support children in coping with everyday emotional challenges. Under the Mask is a fun and accessible way for children to learn practical coping skills, that will serve to be invaluable as they progress through life. Through this intelligent and thoughtful story, the characters have normalised the difficult experiences that can so often isolate a child. As a Mental Health Specialist, I cannot recommend this book enough.'
- Linda Hogan, Occupational Therapist

Printed in Poland
by Amazon Fulfillment
Poland Sp. z o.o., Wrocław

59059122R00019